HAL LEONARD GUITAR METHOD

R&B GUITAR SONGS

ISBN 978-1-4584-2489-1

HAL•LEONARD® CORPORATION
7777 W. BLUEMOUND RD. P.O. BOX 13819 MILWAUKEE, WI 53213

Visit Hal Leonard Online at
www.halleonard.com

Brick House

Words and Music by Lionel Richie, Ronald LaPread, Walter Orange, Milan Williams, Thomas McClary and William King

Intro
Moderately ♩ = 102

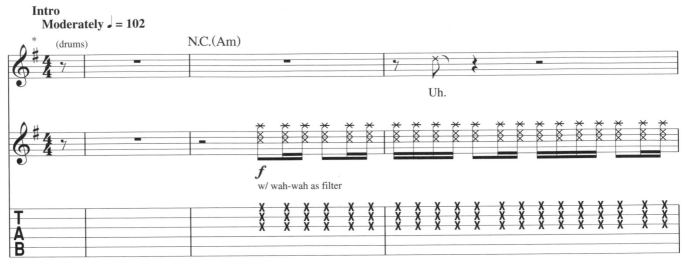

*Key signature denotes A Dorian.

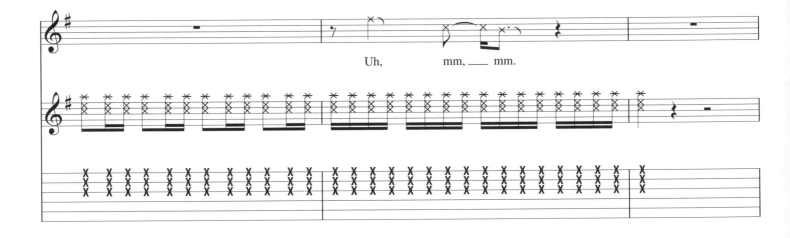

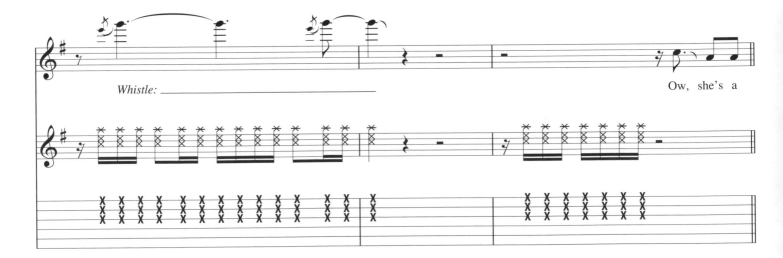

Chorus

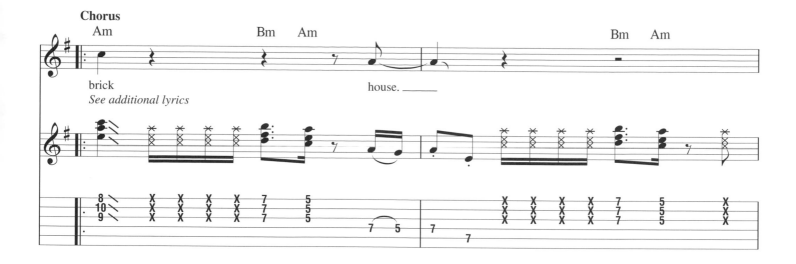

brick house.
See additional lyrics

She's might - y, might - y _____ just let - tin' it all ___ hang out. ___ Ah, she's a

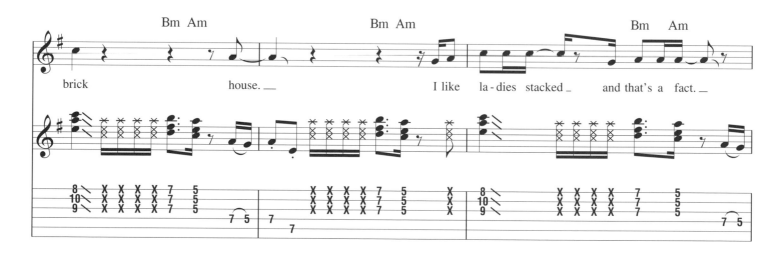

brick house. ___ I like la - dies stacked _ and that's a fact. _

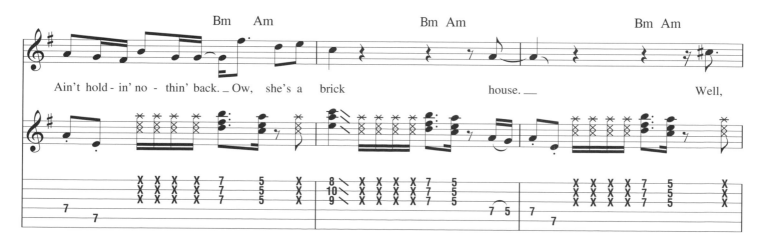

Ain't hold - in' no - thin' back. _ Ow, she's a brick house. ___ Well,

3

Bm   Am   Bm   Am

we're to-geth - er ev-'ry-bod-y knows __ this is how the sto - ry goes. __

Verse

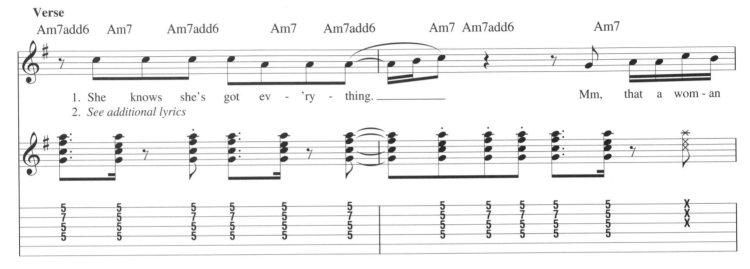

Am7add6 Am7   Am7add6   Am7   Am7add6   Am7 Am7add6   Am7

1. She knows she's got ev-'ry - thing. _____   Mm, that a wom-an
2. *See additional lyrics*

Am7add6 Am7   Am7add6   Am7   Am7add6   Am7

needs   to get a man.   Yeah,   yeah.

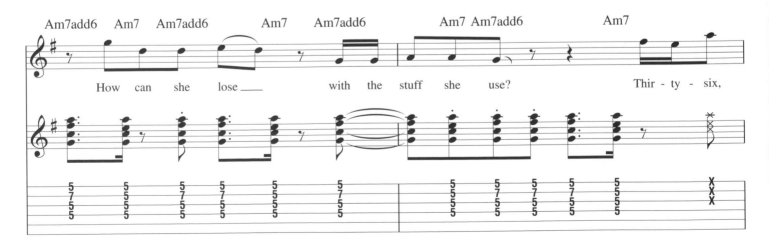

Am7add6 Am7 Am7add6   Am7   Am7add6   Am7 Am7add6   Am7

How can she lose ___   with the stuff she use?   Thir - ty - six,

twen - ty - four,____ thir - ty - six. Ow, what a win - ning hand - ful. She's a

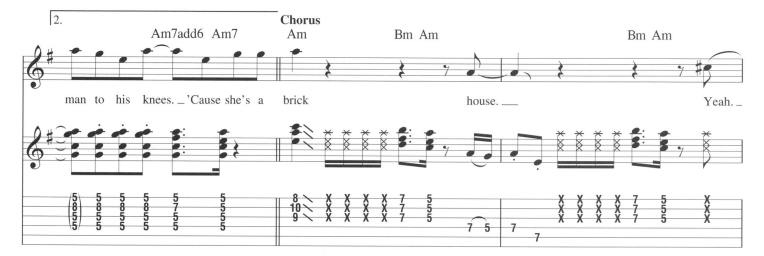

man to his knees. _'Cause she's a brick house. __ Yeah. _

____ she's might - y, might - y ____ just let - tin' it all __ hang out. __ Hey,

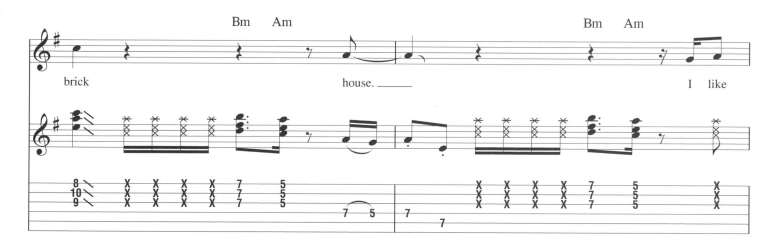

brick house. _____ I like

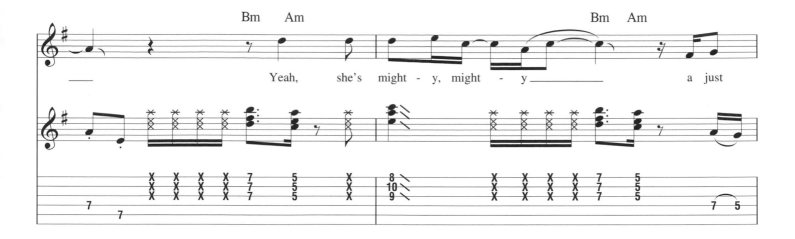

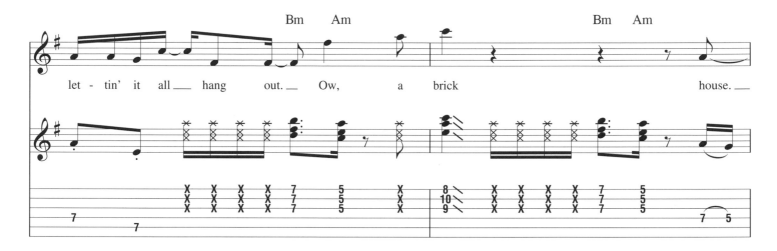

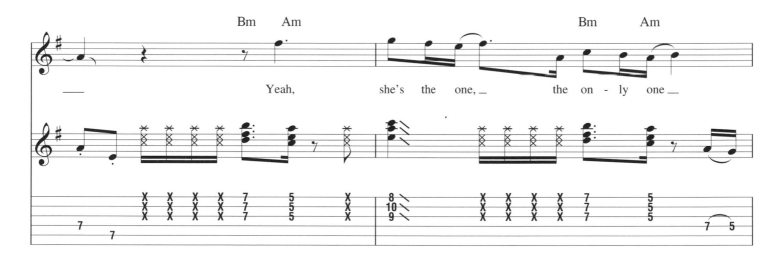

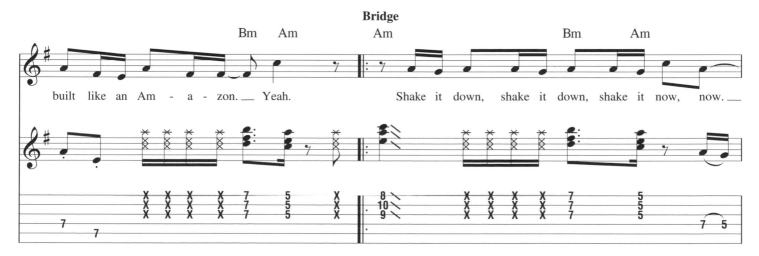

Additional Lyrics

Chorus She's a brick house.
           She's mighty, mighty, just lettin' it all hang out.
           Ah, she's a brick house.
           Oh, I like ladies stacked and that's a fact.
           Ain't holdin' nothin' back.
           Oh, she's a brick house.
           Yeah, she's the one, the only one
           Built like an Amazon.

  2. Mm, the clothes she wear, her sexy ways
     Make an old man wish for younger days, yeah, yeah.
     She knows she's built and knows how to please.
     Sure 'nough can knock a strong man to his knees.

Green Onions

Written by Al Jackson, Jr., Lewis Steinberg, Booker T. Jones and Steve Cropper

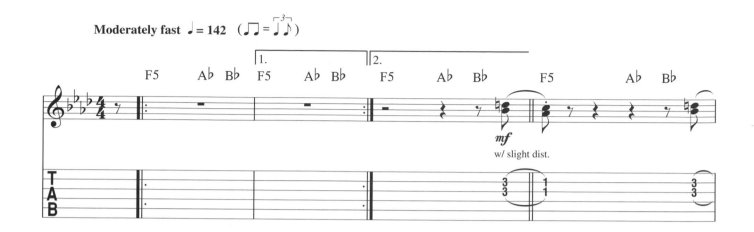

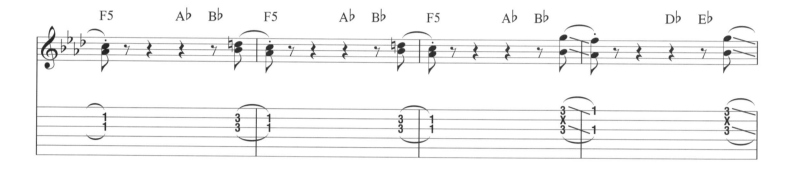

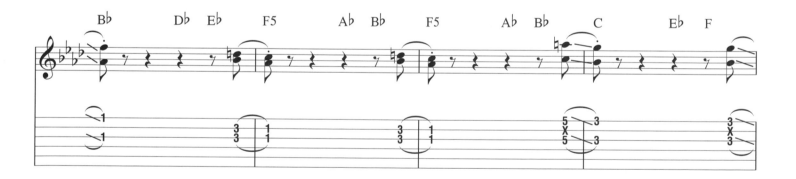

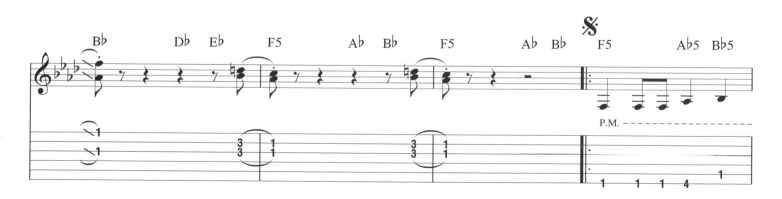

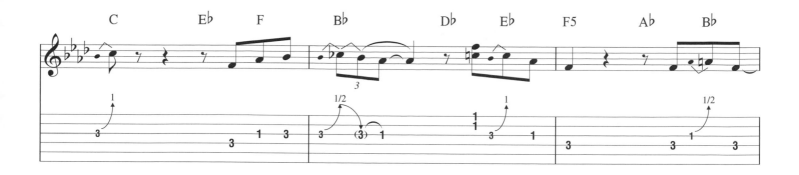

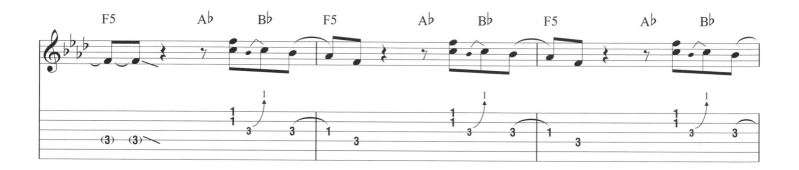

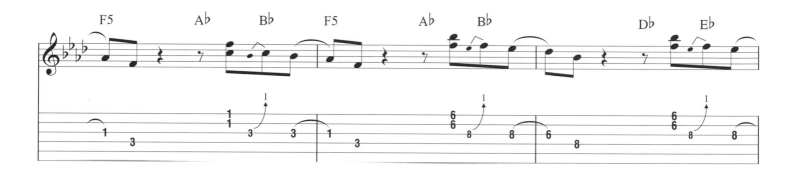

D.S. al Coda
(take repeat)

Coda

Repeat and fade

Outro

Cissy Strut

By Arthur Neville, Leo Nocentelli, George Porter and Joseph Modeliste, Jr.

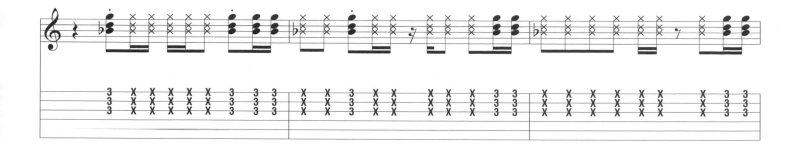

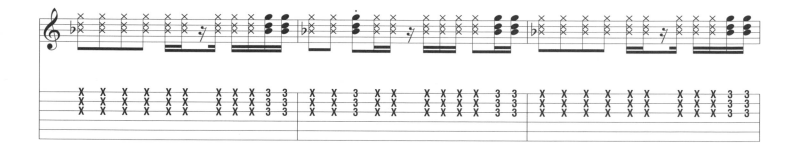

N.C.(C9)

Play 4 times

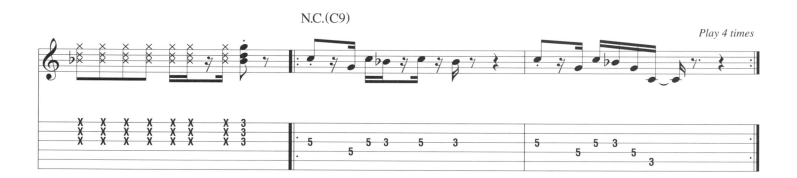

N.C.(C9)   B♭   F   N.C.(C9)

Play 4 times

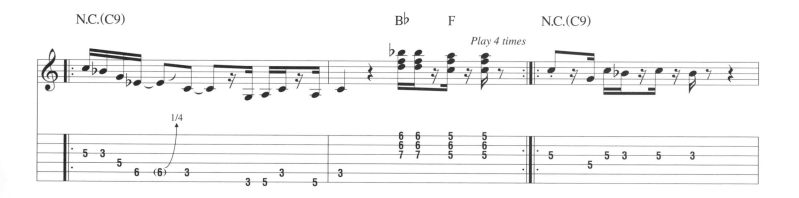

4th time, Begin fade   *Repeat and fade*

N.C.(C9)   B♭   F

Play 4 times

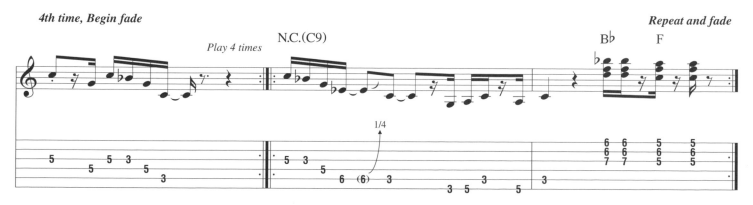

Hold On I'm Comin'

Words and Music by Isaac Hayes and David Porter

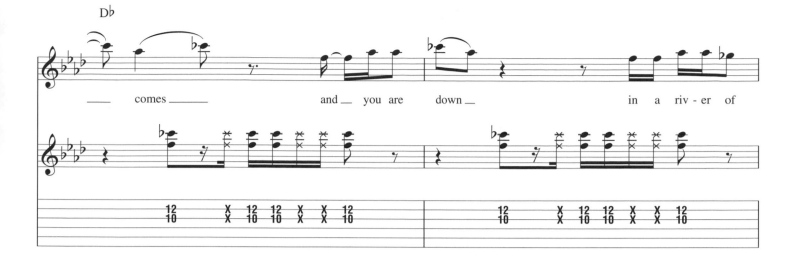

comes _____ and ___ you are down _____ in a riv-er of

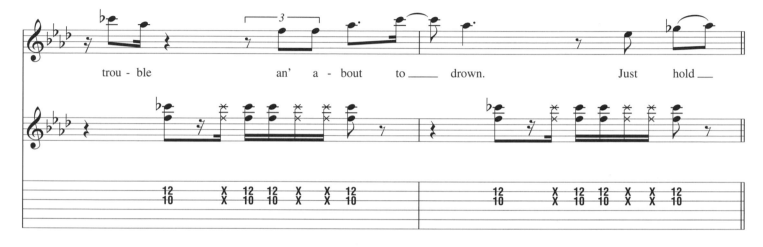

trou-ble   an' a-bout   to _____ drown.   Just hold ___

Chorus

To Coda ⊕

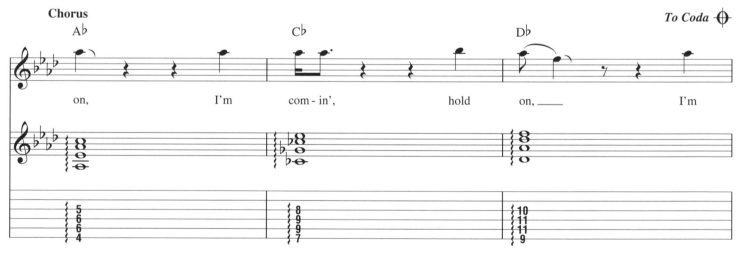

on,   I'm com-in',   hold   on, _____   I'm

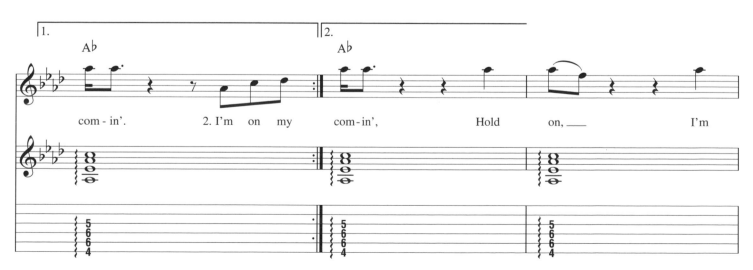

com-in'.   2. I'm on my   com-in',   Hold   on, _____   I'm

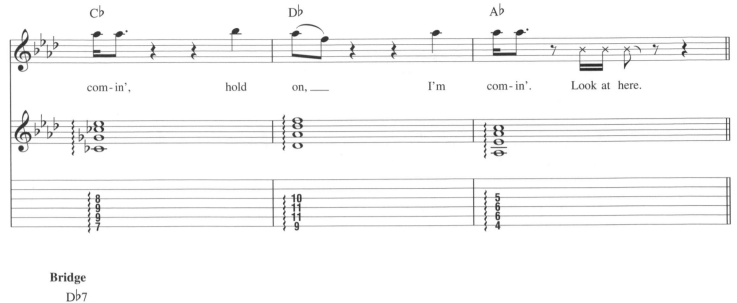

com-in',   hold on, ___   I'm com-in'.   Look at here.

Bridge

Reach   out   to   me   for ___   sat - is - fac -

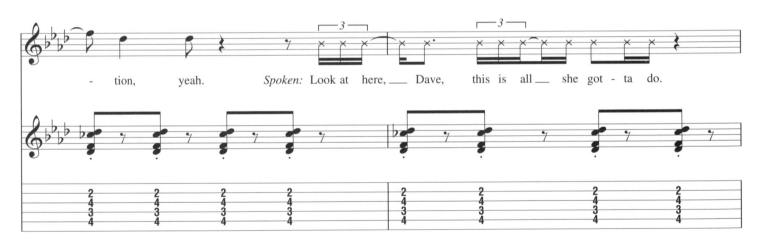

- tion,   yeah.   *Spoken:* Look at   here, ___ Dave,   this is   all ___ she got - ta do.

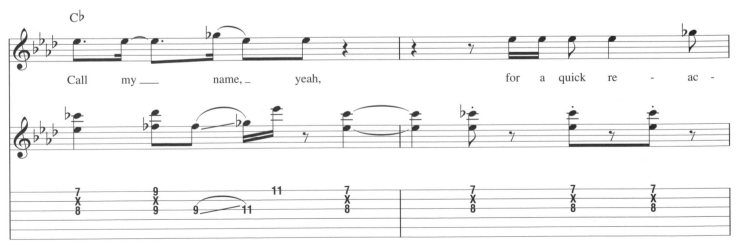

Call   my ___   name, _   yeah,   for   a   quick   re -   ac -

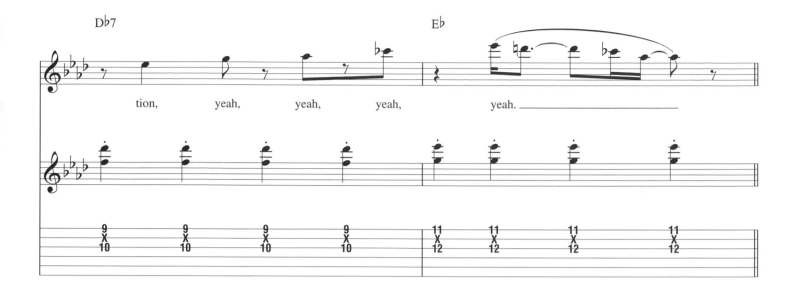

tion,   yeah,   yeah,   yeah,   yeah.

Guitar Solo

Interlude

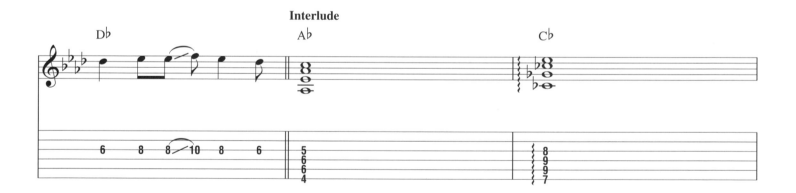

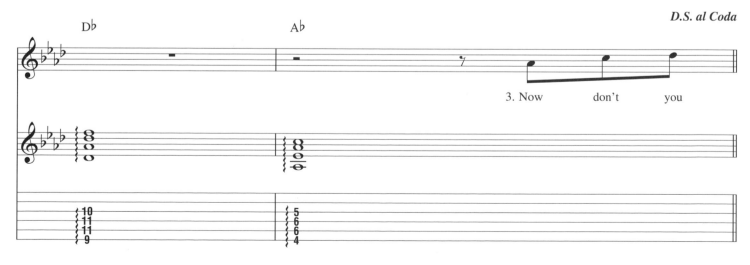

D.S. al Coda

3. Now   don't   you

Additional Lyrics

2. I'm on my way, your lover.
   If you get cold, yeah, I will be your cover.
   Don't have to worry, 'cause I'm here.
   Don't need to suffer, baby, 'cause I'm here.

3. Now don't you ever be sad.
   Lean on me when the times are bad.
   When the day comes and you are down, baby,
   In a river of trouble an' about to drown.

I Just Want to Celebrate

Words and Music by Nick Zesses and Dino Fekaris

Intro
Moderately ♩ = 88

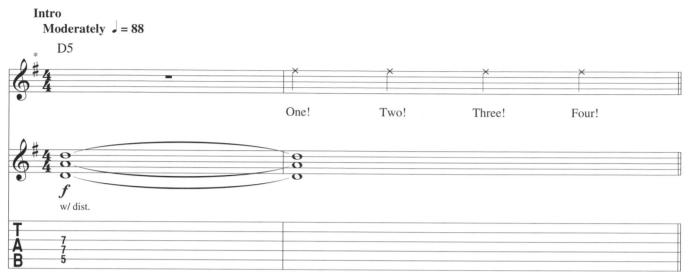

*Key signature denotes D Mixolydian.

Chorus

I just want to cel - e - brate an - oth - er day of liv - in'.

Verse

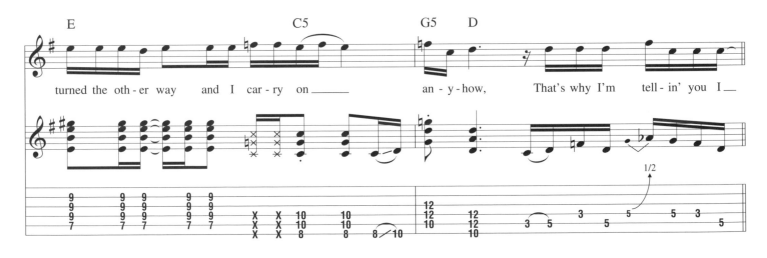

Chorus

I just want to cel - e-brate an - oth-er day of life. _____

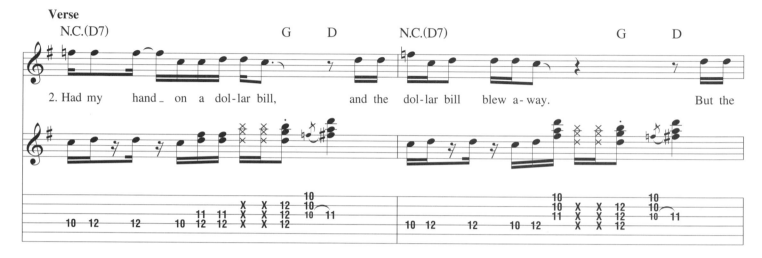

Verse

2. Had my hand _ on a dol-lar bill, and the dol-lar bill blew a-way. But the

sun is shin - in' down _ on me, _ and it's here to stay. That's why I'm tell-in' you I _

Chorus

_ just wan-na cel-e-brate, yeah, yeah, _ an - oth-er day of liv-in'. _____ Yeah, _____

I just want _ to cel - e - brate an - oth - er day _ of liv - in'. Yeah,

I just want _ to cel - e - brate an - oth - er day _ of life. _____

Bridge

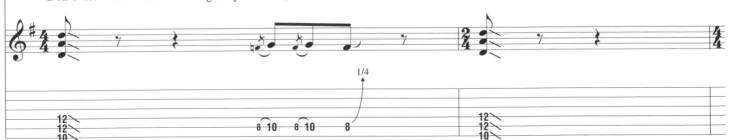

Don't let it all __ get you down, oh no. ___ Don't let it turn _____ you a -

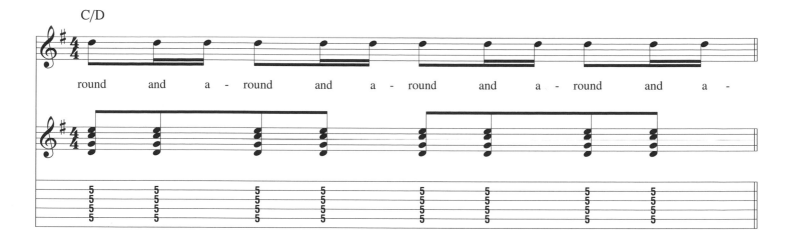

C/D

round and a - round and a - round and a - round and a -

Guitar Solo

N.C.(D7)

round.   3. Well,   I

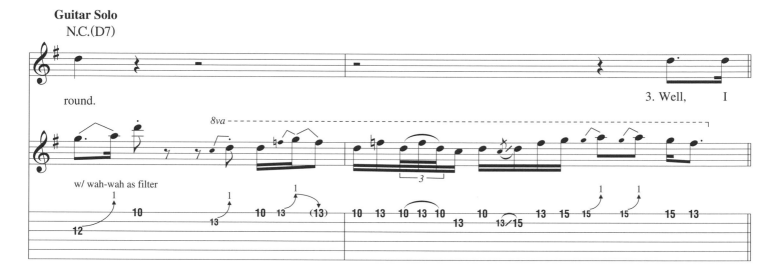

w/ wah-wah as filter

Verse

N.C.(D7)   G   D   N.C.(D7)   G   D

can't be both - ered with sor - row   and I can't _ be both - ered with hate, _ no,   no.   I'm

loco

wah off

E   C5   G5   D

us - in' up my time by feel - in' fine _   ev - 'ry day, __ yeah. That's why I'm   tell - in' you

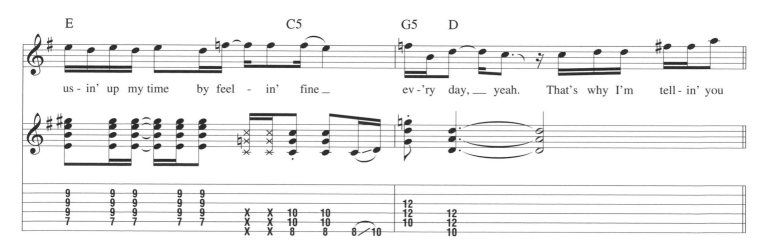

Coda

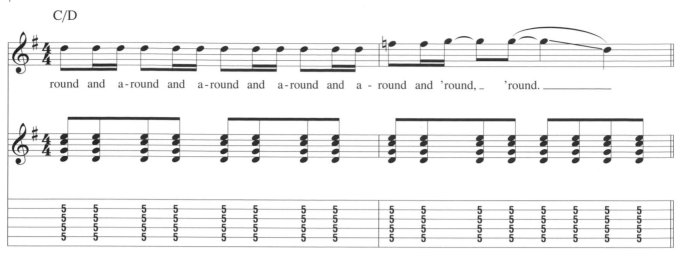

round and a-round and a-round and a-round and a-round and 'round,__ 'round._____

Interlude

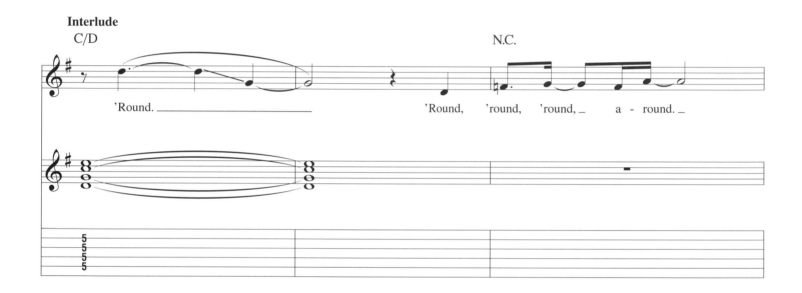

'Round._____ 'Round, 'round, 'round,__ a - round.__

Gtr. tacet

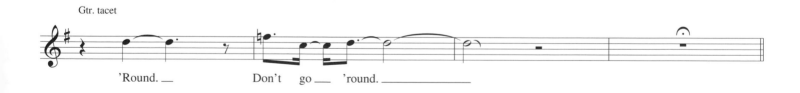

'Round.__ Don't go __ 'round._____

Drum Break   **Outro**   *Repeat and fade*

I_____ just wan - na cel - e - brate._____

I Got You
(I Feel Good)

Words and Music by James Brown

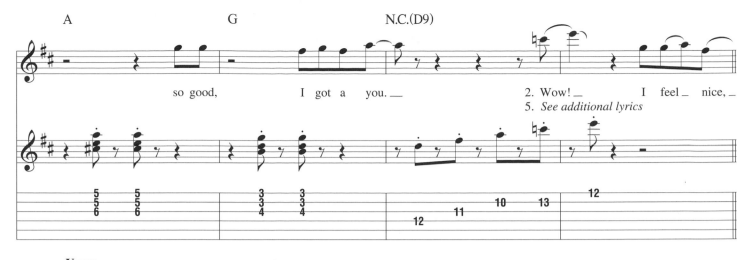

so good, _____ I got a _____ you. _____ 2. Wow! __ I feel __ nice, __

5. *See additional lyrics*

Verse

D7

—____ 2., 3. like sug - ar and spice. _____

G7

I feel _____ nice, _____ like sug - ar and spice. _

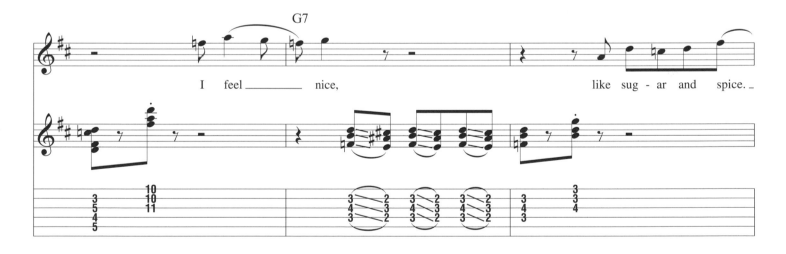

D7

A

—_____ So nice, _____ so nice,

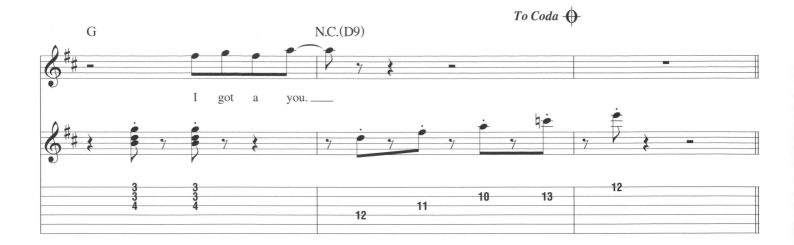

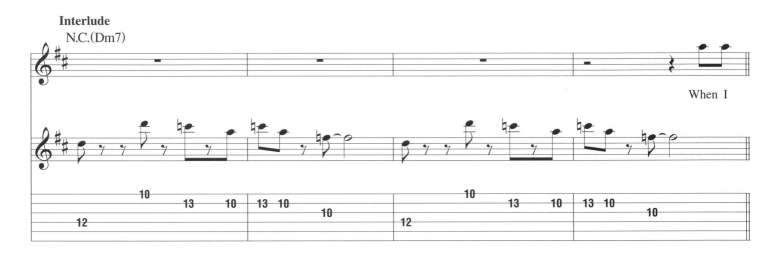

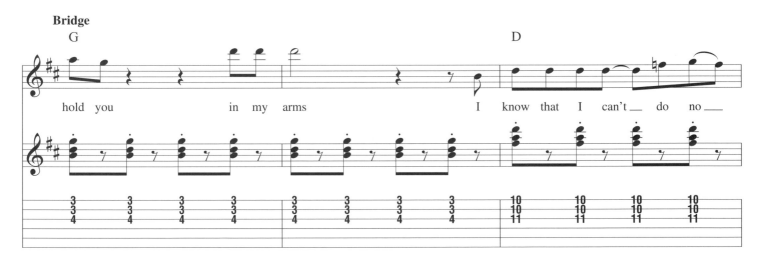

love can't do you no harm.____ 3. And I feel____ ____ 4. And I feel_____

 Coda

So good, so good, 'cause I got a you.____

So good, so good,____ 'cause I got a you.____

slight rit.

slight rit.

Free time

Hey! Ah,____ oo.____

Additional Lyrics

4. And I feel nice,
   Like sugar and spice.
   I feel nice,
   Like sugar and spice.
   So nice, so nice
   That I got a you.

5. Wow! I feel good,
   I knew that I would, now.
   I feel good,
   I knew that I would.
   So good, so good
   That I got a you.

My Girl

Words and Music by William "Smokey" Robinson and Ronald White

Intro
Moderately ♩ = 103

1. I've _ got

Verse

sun - shine _____ on a cloud - y day. ____
2. *See additional lyrics*

When it's cold out - side, _____ I've _ got the

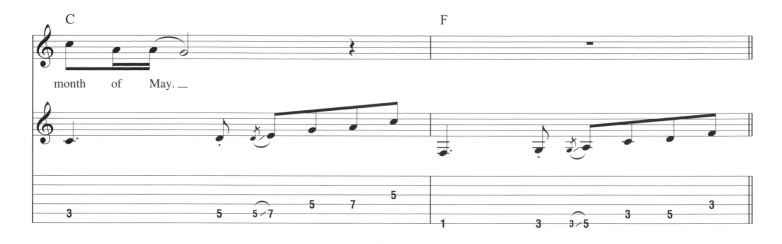

month of May. ___

Chorus

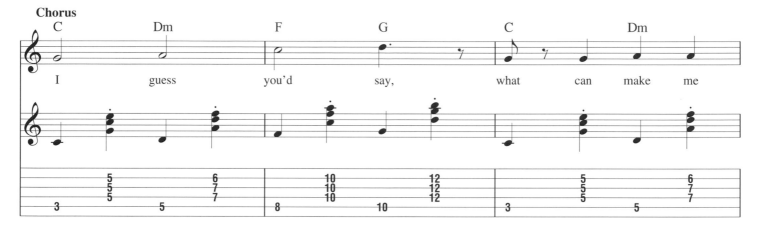

I   guess   you'd   say,   what   can   make   me

feel   this   way? _____   My   girl, _____
                                                    (My   girl.) _____

talk - in' 'bout   my ___ girl, _____   my   girl.   2. I've ___ got
(My   girl.)

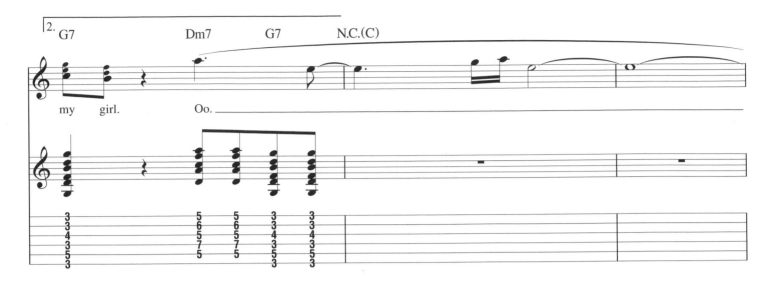

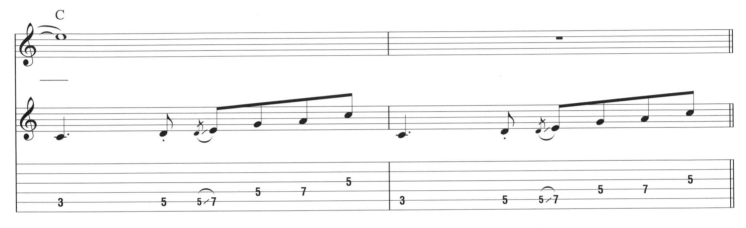

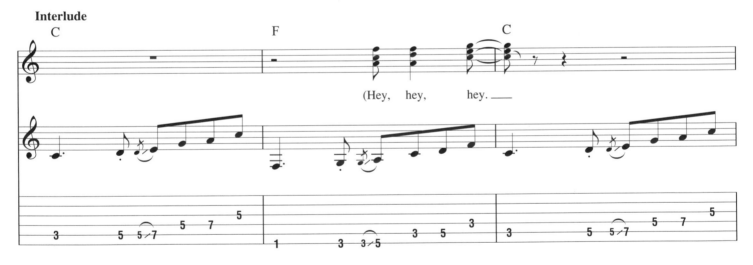

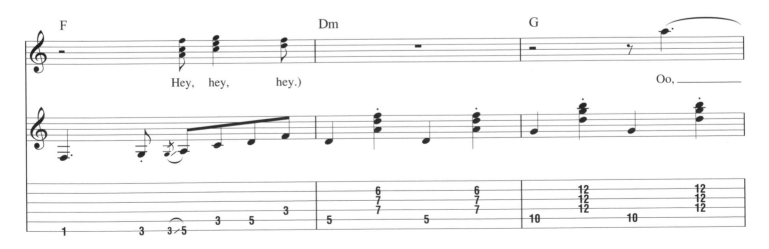

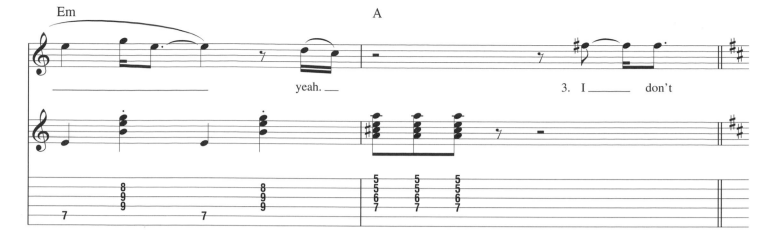

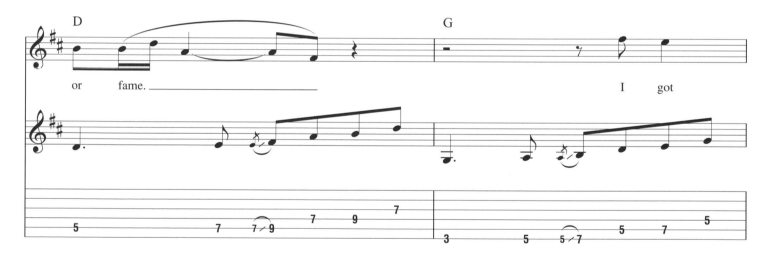

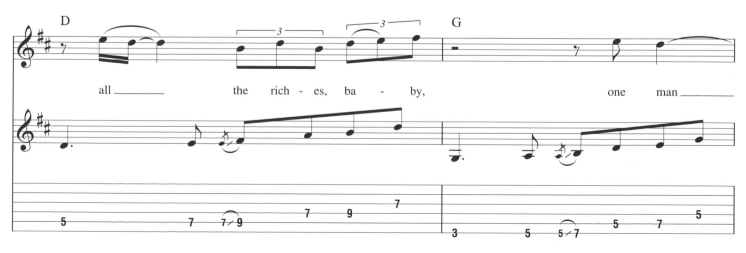

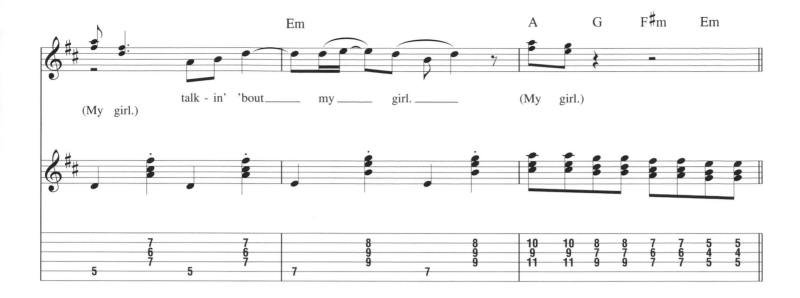

talk - in' 'bout _____ my _____ girl. _____ (My girl.)

(My girl.)

Outro
w/ Voc. ad lib., till fade
Dmaj7

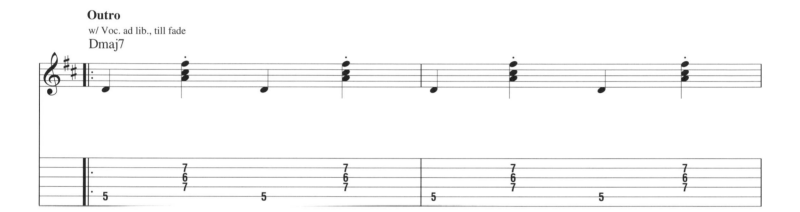

Repeat and fade

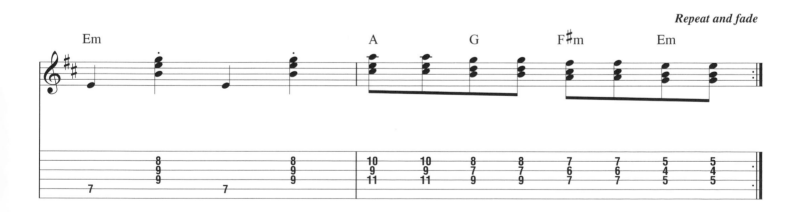

Additional Lyrics

2. I've got so much honey the bees envy me.
I've got a sweeter song than the birds in the tree.

Respect

Words and Music by Otis Redding

Intro
Moderately ♩ = 114

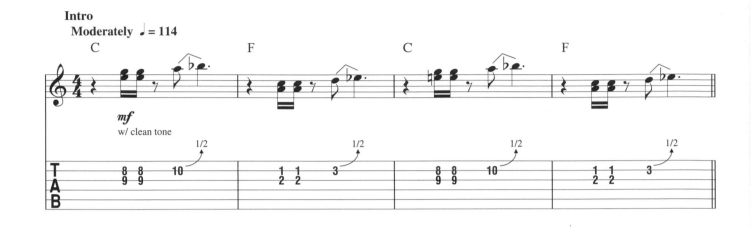

Verse

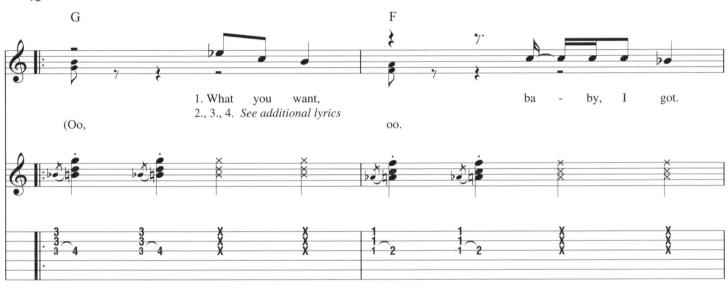

1. What you want, baby, I got.
2., 3., 4. *See additional lyrics*

(Oo, oo.

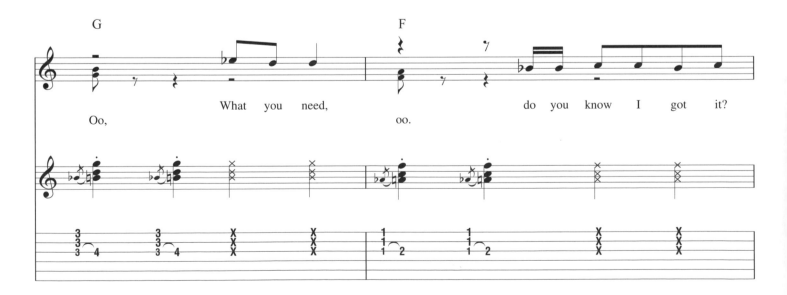

What you need, do you know I got it?

Oo, oo.

All I'm ask - ing　　　　is for a lit - tle re -
Oo,　　　　　　　　oo.

spect when you come home.　　　Hey, __ ba - by.　　When　you come home,
Just a lit - tle bit.　　　　　　　　　　Just a lit - tle bit.

4th time, To Coda ⊕

Just a lit - tle bit.　　　　mis - ter.　　　　Just a lit - tle bit.)

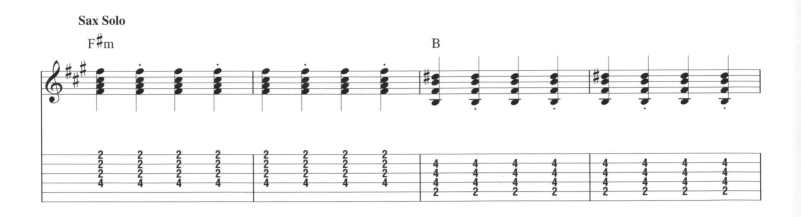

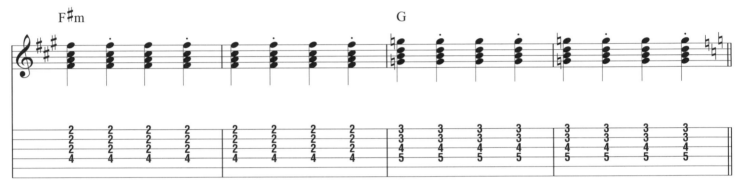

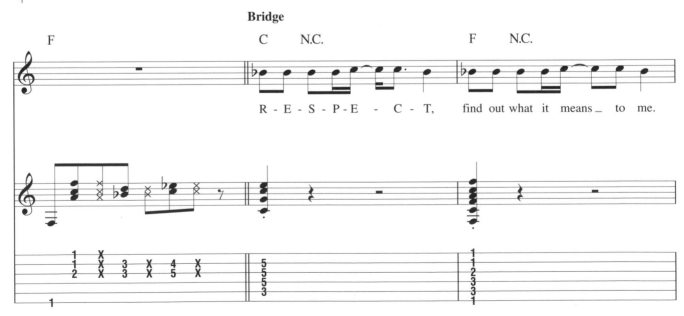

Outro

w/ Voc. ad lib. on repeats

Repeat and fade

Whoa, _____ a lit-tle re - spect.
(Sock it to me, sock it to me, sock it to me, sock it to me. Sock it to me, sock it to me, sock it to me, sock it to me.)

let ring - - - - - - - - - - - - - -

Additional Lyrics

2. I ain't gonna do you wrong while you're gone.
   I ain't gonna do you wrong, 'cause I don't wanna.
   All I'm askin' is for a little respect when you come home.
   Baby, when you get home. Yeah.

3. I'm out to give you all of my money.
   But all I'm askin' in return, honey,
   Is to give me my propers when you get home.
   Yeah, baby, when you get home. Yeah.

4. Oo, your kisses, sweeter than honey.
   But guess what? So is my money.
   All I want you to do for me is give it to me when you get home.
   Yeah, baby, whip it to me when you get home. Now.

Who's Making Love

Words and Music by Bettye Crutcher, Don Davis, Homer Banks and Raymond Jackson

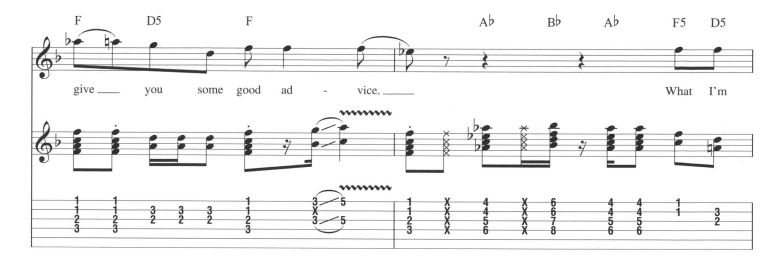

give ___ you some good ad - vice. ___ What I'm

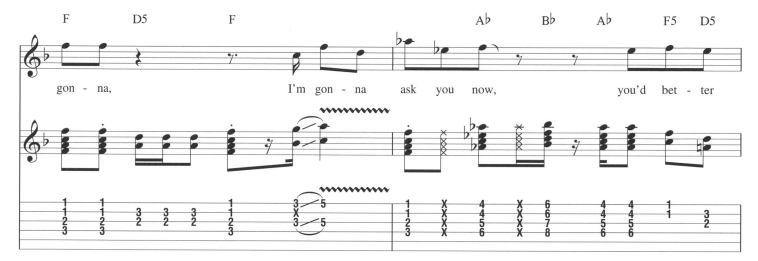

gon - na, I'm gon - na ask you now, you'd bet - ter

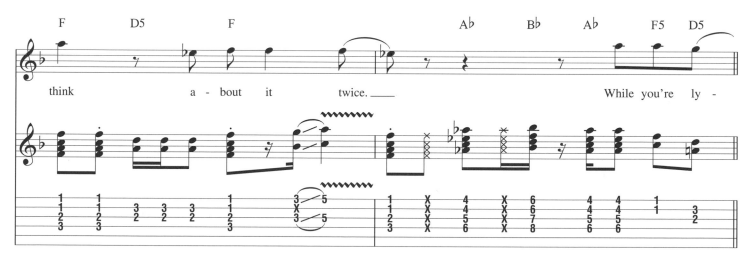

think a - bout it twice. ___ While you're ly -

Pre-Chorus

- in', ___ cheat - in' on your wom - an, there is

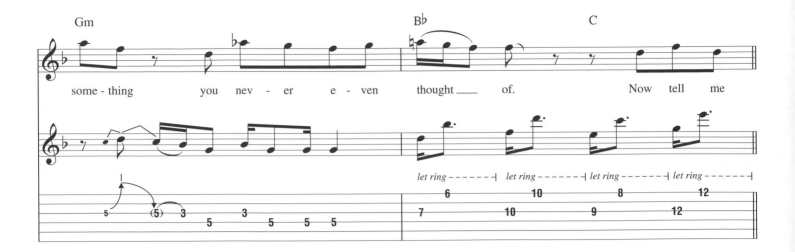

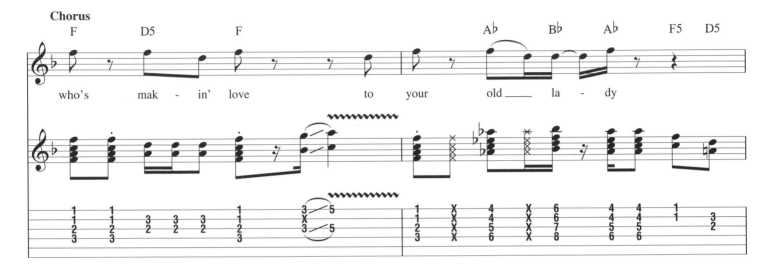

Chorus

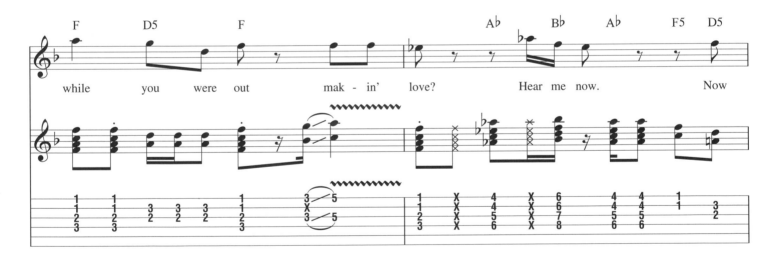

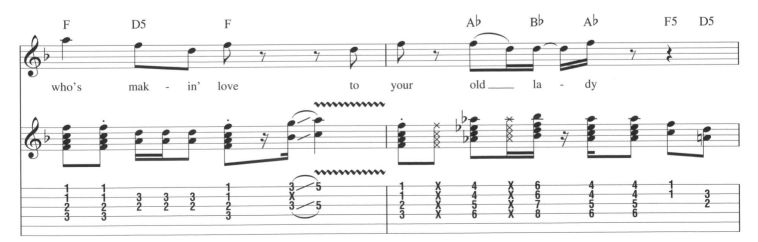

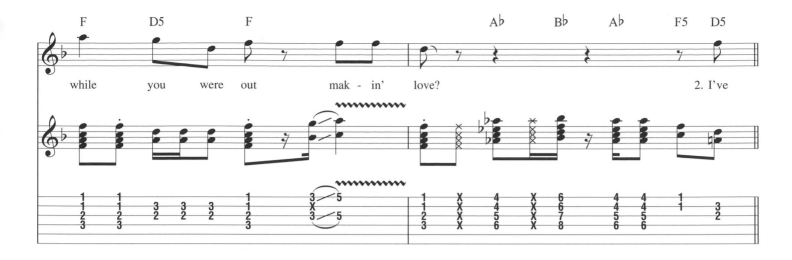

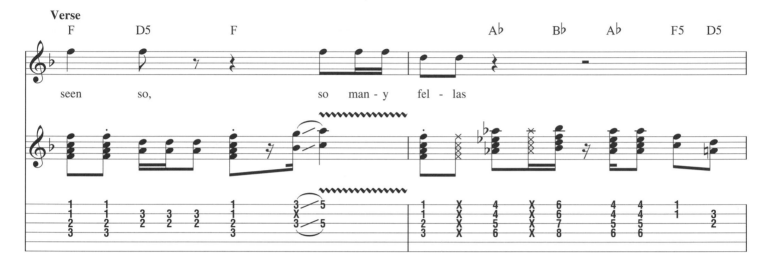

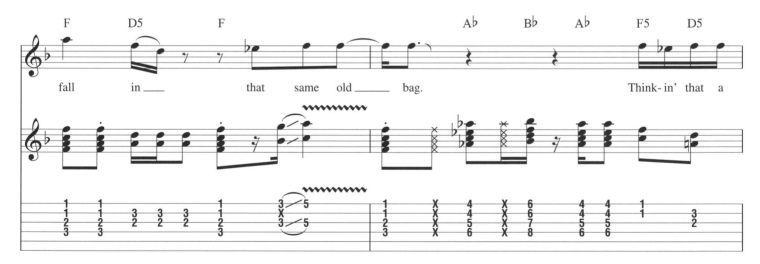

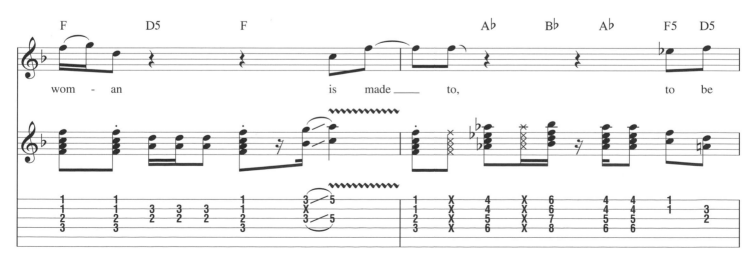

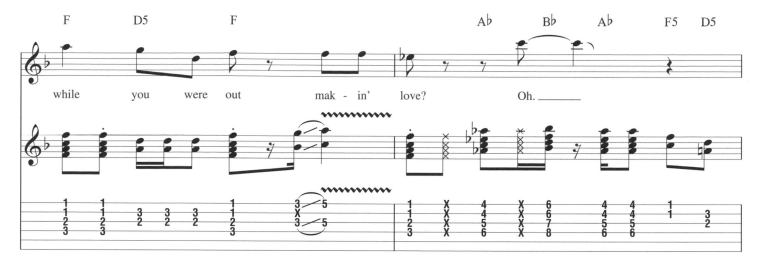

while you were out mak - in' love? Oh. _____

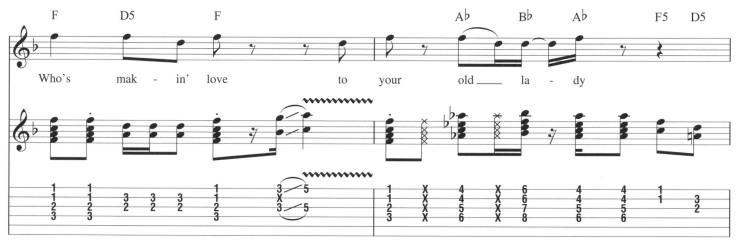

Who's mak - in' love to your old ____ la - dy

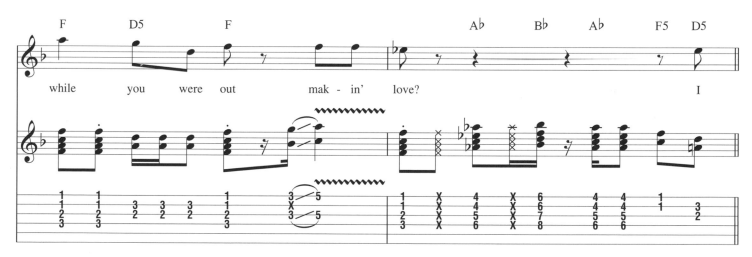

while you were out mak - in' love? I

Bridge

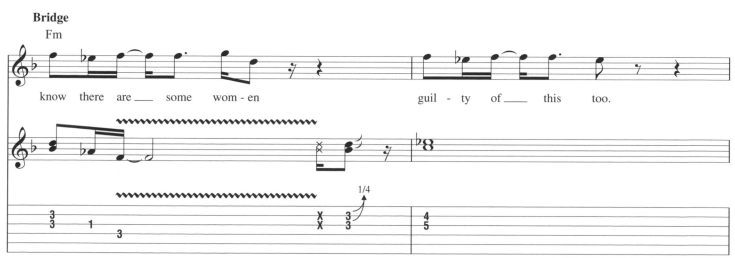

know there are ___ some wom - en guil - ty of ___ this too.

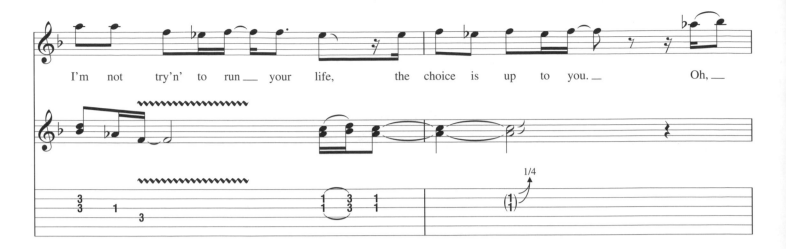

I'm not try'n' to run ___ your life,   the choice is   up   to   you. ___   Oh, ___

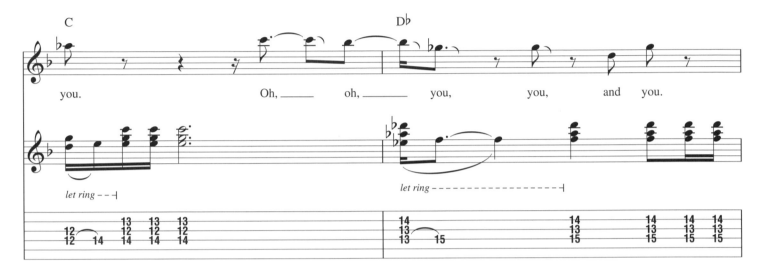

you.   Oh, ___   oh, ___   you,   you,   and   you.

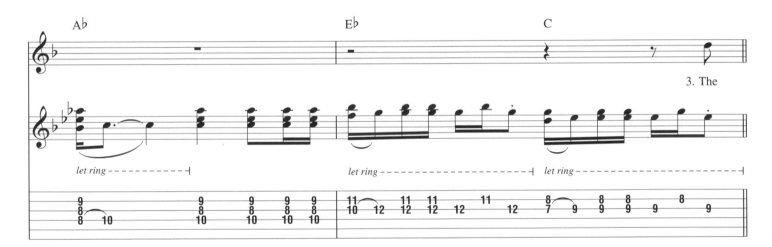

3. The

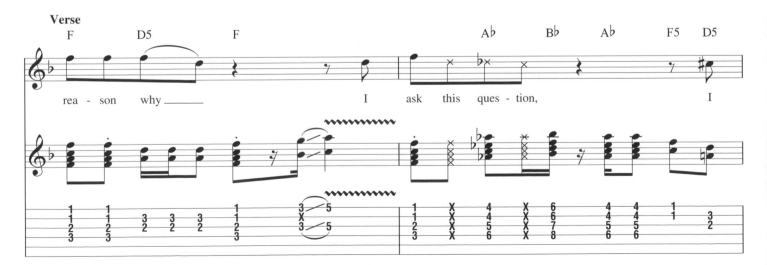

Verse

rea - son   why ___   I   ask   this   ques - tion,   I

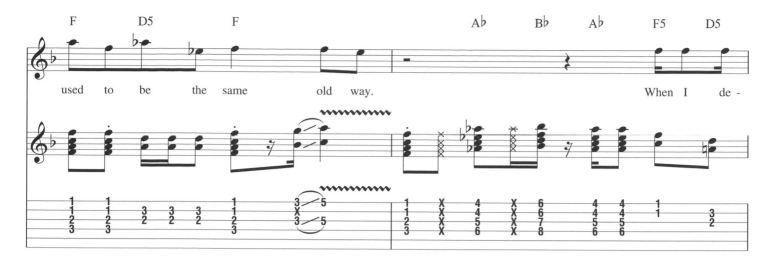

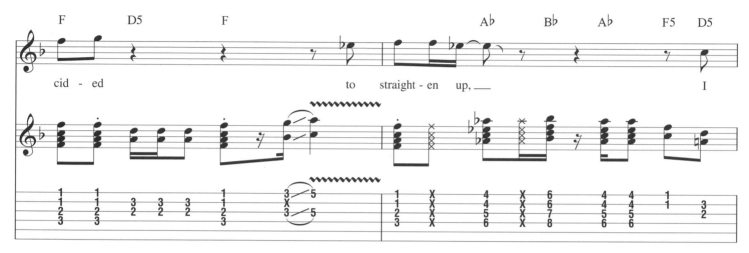

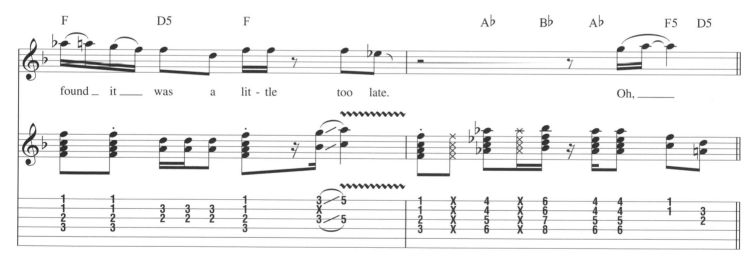

Pre-Chorus

some-thing I nev-er, nev-er dreamed ___ of. Some -

Outro-Chorus

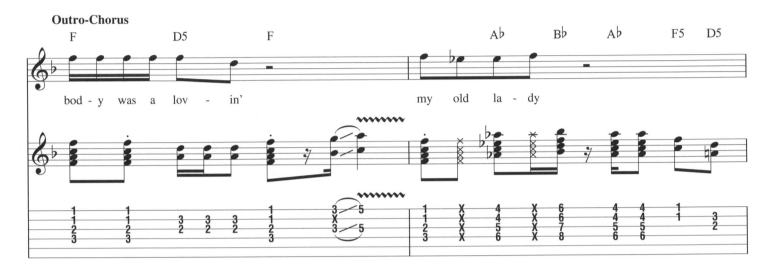

bod-y was a lov-in' my old la-dy

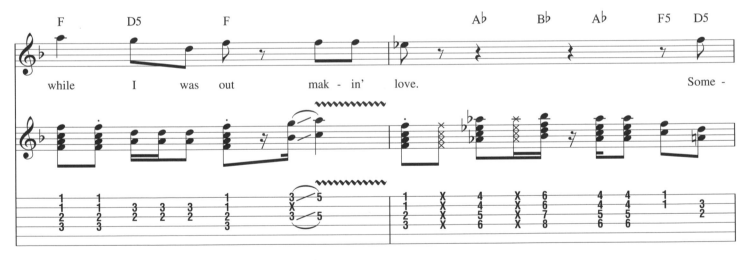

while I was out mak-in' love. Some -

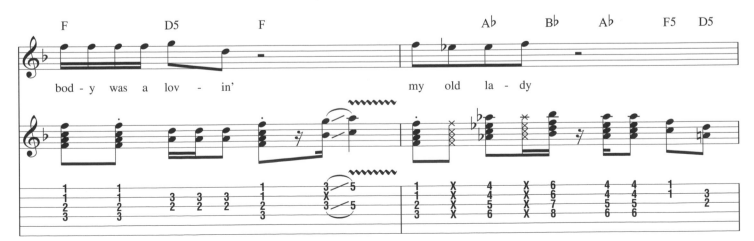

bod-y was a lov-in' my old la-dy

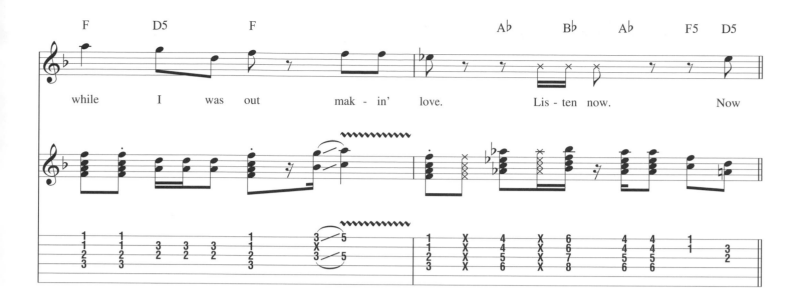

while I was out mak - in' love. Lis - ten now. Now

w/ Voc. ad lib. on repeats

who's mak - ing love to your old ____ la - dy

Repeat and fade

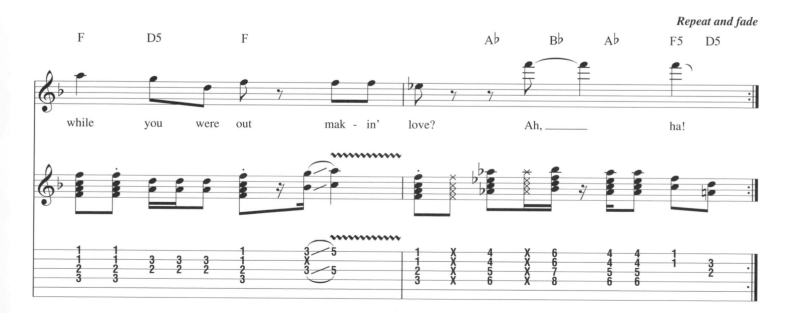

while you were out mak - in' love? Ah, _____ ha!

(Sittin' On) The Dock of the Bay

Words and Music by Steve Cropper and Otis Redding

Verse

left my home ___ in Geor - gia, ___ head - ed for the 'Fris - co Bay. ___

let ring -

___ I have noth-ing to live ___ for, ___ it looks like

let ring -   *let ring -*

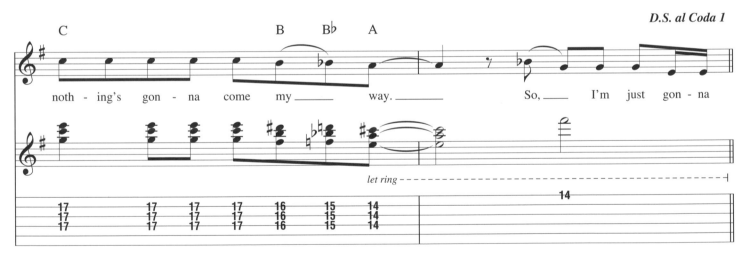

D.S. al Coda 1

noth - ing's gon - na come my ___ way. ___ So, ___ I'm just gon - na

let ring -

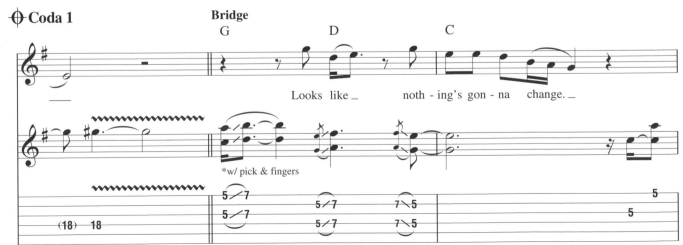

Coda 1

Bridge

Looks like ___ noth - ing's gon - na change. ___

*w/ pick & fingers

*next 8 meas.

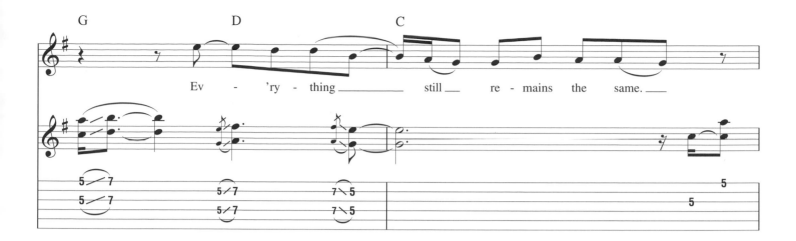

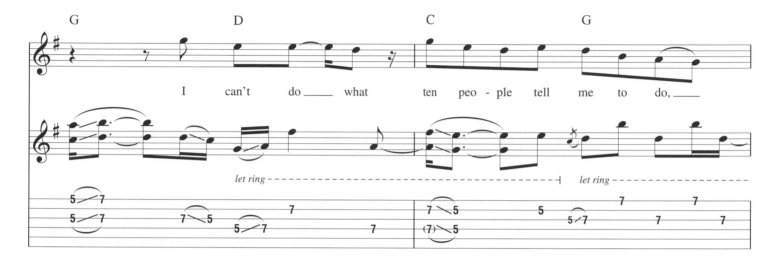

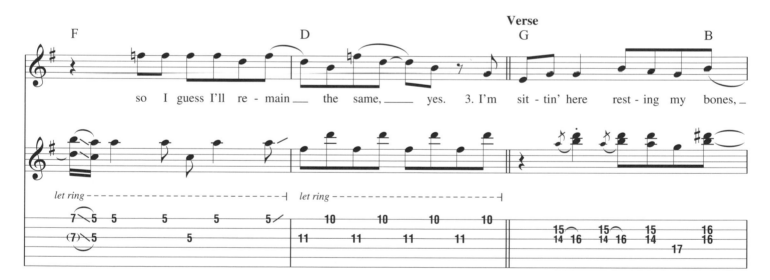

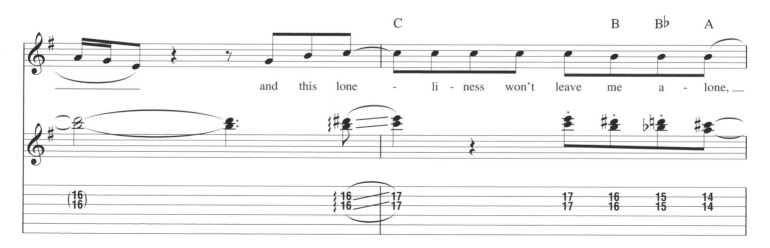

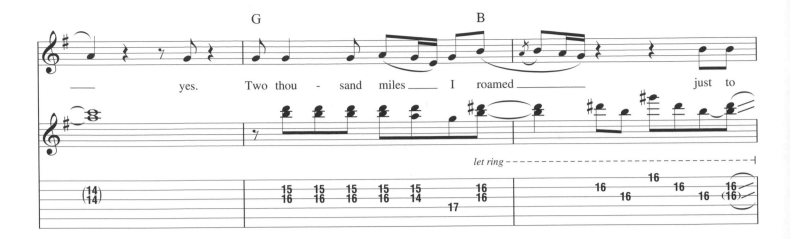

yes. Two thou - sand miles ___ I roamed ___ just to

let ring -

D.S. al Coda 2

make this a dock my ___ home. ___ Now, ___ I'm just gon - na

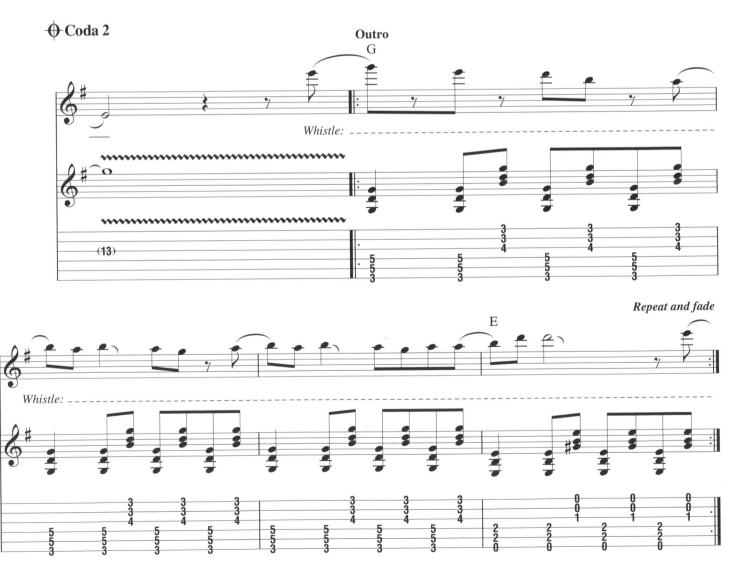

Coda 2

Outro

Whistle: -

Repeat and fade

Whistle: -

GUITAR NOTATION LEGEND

THE MUSICAL STAFF shows pitches and rhythms and is divided by bar lines into measures. Pitches are named after the first seven letters of the alphabet.

TABLATURE graphically represents the guitar fingerboard. Each horizontal line represents a string, and each number represents a fret.

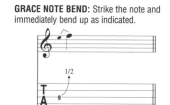

4th string, 2nd fret · 1st & 2nd strings open, played together · open D chord

HALF-STEP BEND: Strike the note and bend up 1/2 step.

WHOLE-STEP BEND: Strike the note and bend up one step.

GRACE NOTE BEND: Strike the note and immediately bend up as indicated.

SLIGHT (MICROTONE) BEND: Strike the note and bend up 1/4 step.

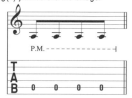

BEND AND RELEASE: Strike the note and bend up as indicated, then release back to the original note. Only the first note is struck.

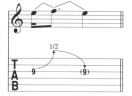

PRE-BEND: Bend the note as indicated, then strike it.

VIBRATO: The string is vibrated by rapidly bending and releasing the note with the fretting hand.

PALM MUTING: The note is partially muted by the pick hand lightly touching the string(s) just before the bridge.

HAMMER-ON: Strike the first (lower) note with one finger, then sound the higher note (on the same string) with another finger by fretting it without picking.

PULL-OFF: Place both fingers on the notes to be sounded. Strike the first note and without picking, pull the finger off to sound the second (lower) note.

LEGATO SLIDE: Strike the first note and then slide the same fret-hand finger up or down to the second note. The second note is not struck.

SHIFT SLIDE: Same as legato slide, except the second note is struck.

TRILL: Very rapidly alternate between the notes indicated by continuously hammering on and pulling off.

TAPPING: Hammer ("tap") the fret indicated with the pick-hand index or middle finger and pull off to the note fretted by the fret hand.

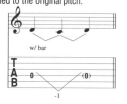

NATURAL HARMONIC: Strike the note while the fret-hand lightly touches the string directly over the fret indicated.

PINCH HARMONIC: The note is fretted normally and a harmonic is produced by adding the edge of the thumb or the tip of the index finger of the pick hand to the normal pick attack.

TREMOLO PICKING: The note is picked as rapidly and continuously as possible.

VIBRATO BAR DIVE AND RETURN: The pitch of the note or chord is dropped a specified number of steps (in rhythm), then returned to the original pitch.

VIBRATO BAR SCOOP: Depress the bar just before striking the note, then quickly release the bar.

VIBRATO BAR DIP: Strike the note and then immediately drop a specified number of steps, then release back to the original pitch.

Additional Musical Definitions

(accent) · Accentuate note (play it louder).

(staccato) · Play the note short.

D.S. al Coda · Go back to the sign (𝄋), then play until the measure marked "***To Coda***," then skip to the section labelled "**Coda**."

D.C. al Fine · Go back to the beginning of the song and play until the measure marked "***Fine***" (end).

Fill · Label used to identify a brief melodic figure which is to be inserted into the arrangement.

N.C. · Harmony is implied.

· Repeat measures between signs.

· When a repeated section has different endings, play the first ending only the first time and the second ending only the second time.

HAL LEONARD **GUITAR METHOD BOOK 1**
SECOND EDITION
CD INCLUDED
BY WILL SCHMID AND GREG KOCH

HAL·LEONARD®

HAL LEONARD GUITAR METHOD

by Will Schmid and Greg Koch

THE HAL LEONARD GUITAR METHOD is designed for anyone just learning to play acoustic or electric guitar. It is based on years of teaching guitar students of all ages, and it also reflects some of the best guitar teaching ideas from around the world. This comprehensive method includes: A learning sequence carefully paced with clear instructions; popular songs which increase the incentive to learn to play; versatility – can be used as self-instruction or with a teacher; audio accompaniments so that students have fun and sound great while practicing.

BOOK 1
Book 1 provides beginning instruction which includes tuning, playing position, musical symbols, notes in first position, the C, G, G7, D, D7, A7, and Em chords, rhythms through eighth notes, strumming and picking, 100 great songs, riffs, and examples. Includes a chord chart and well-known songs: Ode to Joy • Rockin' Robin • Greensleeves • Give My Regards to Broadway • Time Is on My Side.
00699010 Book $6.99
00699027 Book/CD Pack $10.99

BOOK 2
Book 2 continues the instruction started in Book 1 and covers: Am, Dm, A, E, F and B7 chords; power chords; finger-style guitar; syncopations, dotted rhythms, and triplets; Carter style solos; bass runs; pentatonic scales; improvising; tablature; 92 great songs, riffs and examples; notes in first and second position; and more! The CD includes 57 full-band tracks.
00699020 Book $6.99
00697313 Book/CD Pack $9.99

BOOK 3
Book 3 covers: the major, minor, pentatonic, and chromatic scales, sixteenth notes; barre chords; drop D tuning; movable scales; notes in fifth position; slides, hammer-ons, pull-offs, and string bends; chord construction; gear; 90 great songs, riffs, and examples; and more! The CD includes 61 full-band tracks.
00699030 Book $6.99
00697316 Book/CD Pack $9.95

COMPOSITE
Books 1, 2, and 3 bound together in an easy-to-use spiral binding.
00699040 Books Only $14.99
00697342 Book/3-CD Pack $24.99

DVD
FOR THE BEGINNING ELECTRIC
OR ACOUSTIC GUITARIST
00697318 DVD $19.95
00697341 Book/CD Pack and DVD $24.99

SONGBOOKS

EASY POP CHRISTMAS MELODIES
00697417 Book $6.99
00697416 Book/CD Pack $14.99

EASY POP RHYTHMS
00697336 Book $6.95
00697309 Book/CD Pack $14.99

MORE EASY POP RHYTHMS
00697338 Book $6.95
00697322 Book/CD Pack $14.95

EVEN MORE EASY POP RHYTHMS
00697340 Book $6.95
00697323 Book/CD Pack $14.95

EASY POP MELODIES
00697281 Book $6.99
00697268 Book/CD Pack $14.99

MORE EASY POP MELODIES
00697280 Book $6.99
00697269 Book/CD Pack $14.99

EVEN MORE EASY POP MELODIES
00699154 Book $6.95
00697270 Book/CD Pack $14.99

EASY SOLO GUITAR PIECES
00110407 Book $9.99

LEAD LICKS
00697345 Book/CD Pack..$9.99

RHYTHM RIFFS
00697346 Book/CD Pack..$9.95

PEDAL STEEL GUITAR SONGBOOK
00696450 Book/CD Pack $14.99

STYLISTIC METHODS

ACOUSTIC GUITAR
00697347 Book/CD Pack $16.95
00697384 Acoustic Guitar Songs $14.95

BLUEGRASS GUITAR
00697405 Book/CD Pack $16.99

BLUES GUITAR
00697326 Book/CD Pack $16.99
00697385 Blues Guitar Songs $14.95

BRAZILIAN GUITAR
00697415 Book/CD Pack $14.99

CHRISTIAN GUITAR
00695947 Book/CD Pack $12.99

CLASSICAL GUITAR
00697376 Book/CD Pack $14.99
00697388 Classical Guitar Pieces $9.99

COUNTRY GUITAR
00697337 Book/CD Pack $22.99
00697400 Country Guitar Songs $14.99

FINGERSTYLE GUITAR
00697378 Book/CD Pack $17.99

FLAMENCO GUITAR
00697363 Book/CD Pack $14.99

FOLK GUITAR
00697414 Book/CD Pack $14.99

JAZZ GUITAR
00695359 Book/CD Pack $19.99
00697386 Jazz Guitar Songs $14.95

JAZZ-ROCK FUSION
00697387 Book/CD Pack $19.99

ROCK GUITAR
00697319 Book/CD Pack $16.95
00697383 Rock Guitar Songs $14.95

ROCKABILLY GUITAR
00697407 Book/CD Pack $16.99

R&B GUITAR
00697356 Book/CD Pack $14.95

REFERENCE

ARPEGGIO FINDER
00697352 6" x 9" Edition $5.99
00697351 9" x 12" Edition $6.99

INCREDIBLE CHORD FINDER
00697200 6" x 9" Edition $5.99
00697208 9" x 12" Edition $6.99

INCREDIBLE SCALE FINDER
00695568 6" x 9" Edition $5.99
00695490 9" x 12" Edition $6.99

GUITAR CHORD, SCALE & ARPEGGIO FINDER
00697410..$19.99

GUITAR SETUP & MAINTENANCE
00697427 6" X 9" Edition $14.99
00697421 9" X 12" Edition $12.99

HAL·LEONARD
CORPORATION
7777 W. BLUEMOUND RD. P.O. BOX 13819 MILWAUKEE, WI 53213